LOVE IS HOME

LOVE IS HOME

Creating a Home with Heart

HERRON

Contents

INTRODUCTION

What do you heart about your home?

So much time is spent at home. It's where we eat, sleep, rest, rejuvenate and entertain. It's where many of life's big decisions are made and memories are created. This book inspires you to build a reciprocal relationship with one of the most significant players in your life by creating a well-cared-for home that loves you back.

To nurture this relationship, identify the possessions that you treasure and add to them in a thoughtful, considered way. You will soon be surrounded by meaningful textures, colours, patterns, materials and objects that you love, enveloping you in feelings of joy, comfort and belonging.

With plenty of ideas for how to decorate each room in the house and display your cherished items, this book will inspire you to let the story of your life enrich your home, so it can become a well-loved space full of heart.

12 steps to a home with heart

1.

SHOW THE LOVE

Home is a place, but it's also a relationship.

Home is the place you return to when you need to feel safe and secure and be nurtured, so, as in any relationship, you need to show it respect. Care for it as you would a loved one. Keep it clean, avoiding mess and clutter, buy it flowers and take care to show it off in its best light. Then you can truly appreciate all it has to offer, setting the foundation for a happy, loved-up home.

2.

KNOW YOUR STYLE, LOVE YOUR STYLE

The more you know, the better it goes.

Figure out the things you love. What are the colours, the shapes, the looks that make you feel happy? Narrow down your top two styles and pinpoint what you love about them - then choose elements of those styles to include in your home. It doesn't have to be all or nothing. You get to decide what's in or out, so your home is only filled with the things you love.

PARIS
FRANCE

3.

HOME IN ON HOME

Curate your home's focal points carefully for maximum love.

Display your favourite items out in the open. Select complementary objects and group them together to create a feature area in the corner of a room, on a coffee table, sideboard or open shelf. Choose artworks that evoke pleasant feelings or recall happy memories.

4.

CREATE NOOKS AND SOUL ZONES

Enable your home to support your needs.

We all need alone time. Make sure there are designated areas throughout your home for quiet individual activities. Create nooks for research or study that are not only functional but also aesthetically pleasing, inviting spaces where you want to spend time. Construct soul zones: places just for you, where you can read, meditate, journal or paint, surrounded by things that make you happy.

5.

PRIORITISE BEAUTY

Don't forget the obvious. A home to fall in love with is a beautiful home.

Make the effort to transform your home into a beautiful space. Conceal utilities such as wires, plug sockets and unsightly switches. Affix labels to jars, and arrange them beautifully on shelves. Add finishing touches like plush headboards and pretty door handles, candles, oil burners and flowers. Invest in beautiful towels and bed linen and don't forget the luxurious throws, cushions and rugs.

6.

GO SPACE BY SPACE

Get intimate with the nooks and crannies of your home and cater to their needs.

No two areas of the home are the same, so treat them individually. Resist making everything uniform, instead, acknowledge your home's many different qualities and create a separate mood and intention for each room and space in the house.

7.

CELEBRATE AND WELCOME EACH DAY

Support your home to put on its best face every day of the week.

Special things don't need to be kept for special occasions; use the best china and luxury towels every day. Display the valuable ornaments, eat by candlelight, dress the door and place a welcome mat at the entrance to your home, injecting love and significance into the ordinary.

8.

EMBRACE NATURE

Nurture the dynamic between your home and its environment.

Create a view within your home, allowing plenty of natural light to filter in through the windows, connecting the interior of your space with the world outside. Display pot plants and flowers and consider including seasonal reminders by arranging fresh fruit and treasures from nature that reflect the shifts and transitions of the year.

PLENTY
STILL

9.

THINK COMFORT AND JOY

How can you add these qualities to your home?

Fill your home with plump cushions and sumptuous throws, beautiful bed linen and fluffy towels: tactile delights that envelop you in warmth. Think scented candles or oil diffusers, beautiful bathroom indulgences and a great sound system to play your favourite music. Display items with sentimental value, handmade ceramics, gifts and travel mementos, and add little details such as coffee coasters or reading lamps that bring a room to life and express your personality.

10.

TELL YOUR STORY AND EXPRESS YOURSELF

A well-loved home is full of stories.

Your home should be reflection of you and the life you have lived. Celebrate your story and all the things that spell love to you. Position yourself through your home by including items that have meaning and sentimental value, such as books and family artefacts, treasured photographs, tokens of affection and holiday mementos.

Dracula
Bram Stoker
Park
Jane Austen
Sensibility
Jane Austen
VIRGINIA WOOLF
A ROOM OF ONE'S OWN
ROBIN HOOD
A MOVE-ABLE FEAST
ERNEST HEMINGWAY
READER'S DIGEST
Best Loved Books
FOR YOUNG READERS
The Scarlet Pimpernel
Tom Sawyer
The Good Earth
Robin Hood
THIS ROUGH MAGIC
MARY STEWART
THE AD-VENTURES OF TOM SAWYER
Twain
BEN HUR
WALLACE
THE HUNCHBACK OF NOT
WHAT KATY DID
by
SUSAN COOLIDGE
DEAN & SON LTD.
ALL THE LIGHT WE CANNOT SEE
ANTHONY DOERR
ABBEY LIBRARY
LIFE OF PI
YANN MARTEL
WATCHING ME WATCHING YOU
FAY WELDON
The Horse Whisperer
NICHOLAS EVANS
IN PURSUIT OF THE ENGLISH
DORIS LESSING
KATE

11.

HONOUR FUNCTION

When our needs are met, we feel happy. Home is no exception to this rule.

A great way to cement your love affair with home is to ensure it works for you. Form and function should come together in every space to create beautiful areas that meet your needs. Think open shelves designed both for storage and display, beautiful folding screens that divide rooms, chic hooks and curtain tie backs that add a sense of style and keep things tidy. When your home is functioning well, it becomes a place where you want to be.

12.

LOVE LIGHTING

Illuminate the love by paying attention to the lighting in your home.

Bring in natural light by replacing heavy drapes with sheer curtains. Pay attention to detail by illuminating specific areas with under-cabinet lighting, wall sconces or tailored lighting to brighten alcoves or nooks.

Create a beautiful ambience using dimmer switches, candles or salt lamps. Avoid harsh overhead light by selecting light shades that gently diffuse the light or opt instead for table lamps and standing lamps to subtly highlight chosen corners and create a softer feel.

CHAPTER 1

Hall & Entry

Welcome the Love

'You're as welcome as the flowers in May and we love you in the same old way.'

HANK SNOW

It's up to you. You can design a space that, when you walk in the door, is welcoming: the feeling of a home that is taken care of, filled with treasured items, exuding love and capturing your personality.

To help achieve this, keep the space free from clutter. Select furniture with diminutive dimensions, a slimline console table, for example, that suits your entryway and does not overcrowd.

Dress up your entryway with a few special mementos; select artworks or ornaments that have sentimental value that you will see every time you walk through the door. Flowers or plants add beauty, vibrancy and freshness, making a house feel like a home.

1. Dress your front door and create a beautiful first impression.

2. Place a welcome mat at the entryway to greet visitors.

3. Show some affection to the hall with elegant rugs or runners.

4. Add personalised touches such as a handmade pot for your keys or an inherited vase.

5. Select attractive storage options that keep things tidy and look appealing.

6. Beautify the space by including large plants with oversized foliage or trailing leaves.

7. Select a suitably sized hall table and dress it with books and personal objects.

8. If space allows, create a nook with a chair or bench.

9. Introduce elements of your style that continue throughout the rest of your home.

10. A mirror and fresh flowers show appreciation and care.

A well-dressed door and an immaculately cared for entryway, complete with lush greenery and chic tiles, make your home feel warm and inviting.

Create a wreath to display on your front door, select distinctive door numbers and paint your door in a colour that you love.

‘A beautiful plant is like a having a friend around the house’

BETH DITTO

Plants either just inside or outside the front door make a strong statement. Subtle foliage or big bold leaves bring a sense of freshness and vibrancy and make the space feel appealing.

Express yourself. Showcase your likes and loves with meaningful treasures such as family photos and a handmade pot for your keys.

HOME
Sweet

WELCOME MAT

A welcome mat is an essential feature of your entryway. It creates an impression, conveying a message to visitors before they enter the house, and even to those who always remain on the threshold (Hi, postie!).

Opt for a style that you love. It can be simple and classic, elegant and beautiful, fun or kid friendly. Whether you want to showcase your sleek style or offer up a touch of humour, go with something that feels good to you.

The great thing about welcome mats is that you can change them regularly if you feel like a freshen up. Add something with a little sparkle or a bold splash of colour, or embrace visitors with a clearly written invitation to enter.

Consider layering your welcome mat on top of a small rug to add personality and another textural element. Mix and match florals and stripes, checks and polka dots to make a real feature of your porch.

A beautiful pot plant or a chic lantern placed next to your doormat can transform the space into something more considered, creating a look that feels complete.

It's essential in this space to have a tidy spot for shoes, coats and bags. Hidden shoe storage can be handy and large wall hooks make a stylish design feature that's functional too.

INTRODUCE YOUR STYLE

Demonstrate your taste and set up the vibe of your home.

The hall and entryway is the perfect place for a statement about your home. First impressions do not get a second chance, so take this opportunity to clearly introduce your style. Think about its character and create a small vignette that alludes to the style of the rest of your home.

Establish the colour palette and consider including some of the textiles, ornaments or artworks that you love. It doesn't have to be a dramatic, over-the-top announcement, just a gentle suggestion, allowing the entryway to your home to become an entryway to your style.

Rugs and runners are costly but worth it if budget allows. A beautiful rug or runner makes a great impression and creates a warm welcome as you enter the home.

‘If you’re waiting for your next love, look in the mirror.’

BRIDGETT DEVOUE

A mirror for that quick check before leaving home is essential in any entryway. Add a plant or fresh flowers for a little extra something that looks good too.

A nook with a chair or bench is lovely in your entryway areas; somewhere to sit and put on shoes or just unwind for five minutes before or after a busy day.

If space allows, a hall table (specially designed to fit the slimmer space of a hallway) is decorative and functional. The perfect place to store your keys and wallet, it can even be used to divide the space.

TOGETHER

CHAPTER 2

Living

Express Yourself

‘Home is where love resides, memories are created, friends always belong, and laughter never ends.’

ANONYMOUS

The living room is comfort-central of the home, a place to nestle in and get cosy, relax and unwind. Consider how you arrange your furniture and try to bring it in close so that it feels intimate and creates a sense of togetherness.

Choose fabrics that are soft and luxurious; plenty of plush cushions and throws make for a sensory delight.

Avoid overcrowding surfaces, which can feel cluttered. Instead, choose with care a few select items that mean love to you: objects that have been cherished or that represent a connection to family or special memories.

Welcome in as much natural light as possible to boost your body’s feel-good hormones, and don’t forget the houseplants for added vitality and energy, helping to purify the air and nourish the space.

1. Love and respect your existing belongings. Say thanks for what you have.

2. Display mementos from your family and life story so far.

3. Create groupings of loved items.

4. Subtly introduce the theme of love through your choice of artwork and objects that you display, but try not to go over the top.

5. Conceal utilities to create an aura of simplicity, beauty and ambience.

6. Create a soul zone; a tranquil space for alone time.

7. Consider open shelves to display your treasured and much loved possessions.

8. Bring furniture in and away from the walls to create intimate spaces where everything is within reach.

9. Display photos of loved ones, loved things and special events.

10. Welcome in warmth and personality through use of pattern.

> 'Where we love is home, home that our feet may leave, but not our hearts.'
>
> OLIVER WENDELL HOLMES SR

Bring in the love by choosing artworks, ornaments or furnishings that feature love-related motifs like hearts or affirmations. But don't overdo it. A few well-chosen pieces is sweet. Too many can get cheesy quickly.

START WHERE YOU ARE

Give thanks for your home and conduct an 'appreciation audit' to remind yourself of everything there is to love.

Remember, not everything has to be shiny and new. Your budget may not allow you to replace everything in your home, nor is it necessary. Take a good look around at all the things you already own. Select special pieces to keep that evoke sentimental feelings, and remove items that no longer serve you. Well-loved belongings and those with a rich history are a part of the joy and character of home.

In your living spaces include artefacts from family archives and mementos from your travels - things that remind you of your story; who you are, where you've come from and where you've been.

Use open shelving to place your special items on display, arranged in clusters.

Hang family portraits and photographs as an everyday reminder of love and gratitude for the special people and moments in your life.

Feel the love with layer upon layer of soft textures, sumptuous throws, plush cushions and rich textiles.

Conceal utilities like light switches and unsightly wires. Add in functional-but-beautiful touches like vented screens and curtain tie-backs to ensure a calm, streamlined space.

Create soul zones where you can retreat to nourish yourself: areas designed specifically for the activities that you love. Perhaps a cosy nook for curling up with a good book or a beautiful desk in an alcove, perfect for painting or writing.

LOVE PATTERN

Weave love into your home furnishings by selecting patterns that relate to your life story. Choose images and shapes that represent fond memories or that capture some of the day-to-day things in life that make you happy.

A floral motif for curtains could contain an image of a flower that you were given on a special occasion, a detailed throw may be reminiscent of your favourite book cover, or wallpaper may evoke a design similar to that of your grandparents' crockery. A soft wave or striking geometrical pattern on a cushion evokes the ocean or mountain ranges, reminding you of your love for these places.

There are other ways to use pattern to conjure up emotions. Consider how the shapes of your space relate. From the placements of books on a shelf and the layout of floorboards or furniture to the knots and burls visible in timber pieces, think about how everything works together and how you can create a space that is harmonious and endearing.

Photographs or artworks displayed in a pattern that is striking and aesthetically pleasing allow your eyes to easily flow across the images and create the sense of a space that is cherished.

Come closer, my love. If space allows, keep furniture away from walls, at least 150mm, but more is even nicer.

Make use of leftover spaces. Place a bench seat, ottoman or console unit behind the sofa; a large plant or selection of plants in a corner; divide up the space with a well-styled table; or create a secondary seating area with a window seat or a pile of poufs and floor cushions.

CHAPTER 3

Sleeping

Love and Be Loved

The bedroom is the place to enshrine the love in your home. And to feel rested and loved.

Create a space that is perfect for sleep and a dream to retreat to at the end of the day. Keeping it clean and clear helps reduce the internal chatter and busyness that goes along with cluttered spaces, and instead establishes a sanctuary of calm.

Distribute soft touches all around the room, not solely on the bed. Select plush cushions and thick rugs, an upholstered chair and gorgeous throws. Lean towards richer, more luxurious fabrics for a sensuous delight that invites caress.

Select an artwork that sets up the mood of your space and remember to add a touch of greenery to bring in life and vitality.

Layer your lighting to create an intimate ambience. Limit bright overhead lighting and opt instead for filtered natural light through sheer curtains, delicate wall scones, floor and table lamps and the warming glow of candlelight.

1. Love your pillows and they will love you back. Choose carefully.

2. Pay attention to your bedside table.

3. Introduce personal touches. Celebrate your love story.

4. Choose the softest, most luxurious bed linen you can afford.

5. Be prepared to adjust your sleeping environment according to the seasons.

6. Add greenery.

7. Ensure that you have a place for all the things. Aim for clutter-free love.

8. Create a view, even if you don't have one.

9. Love your lighting - it's key to a beautiful space.

10. Go beyond your comfort zone. Consider darker colours and richer finishes or lavish elements in your preferred design style.

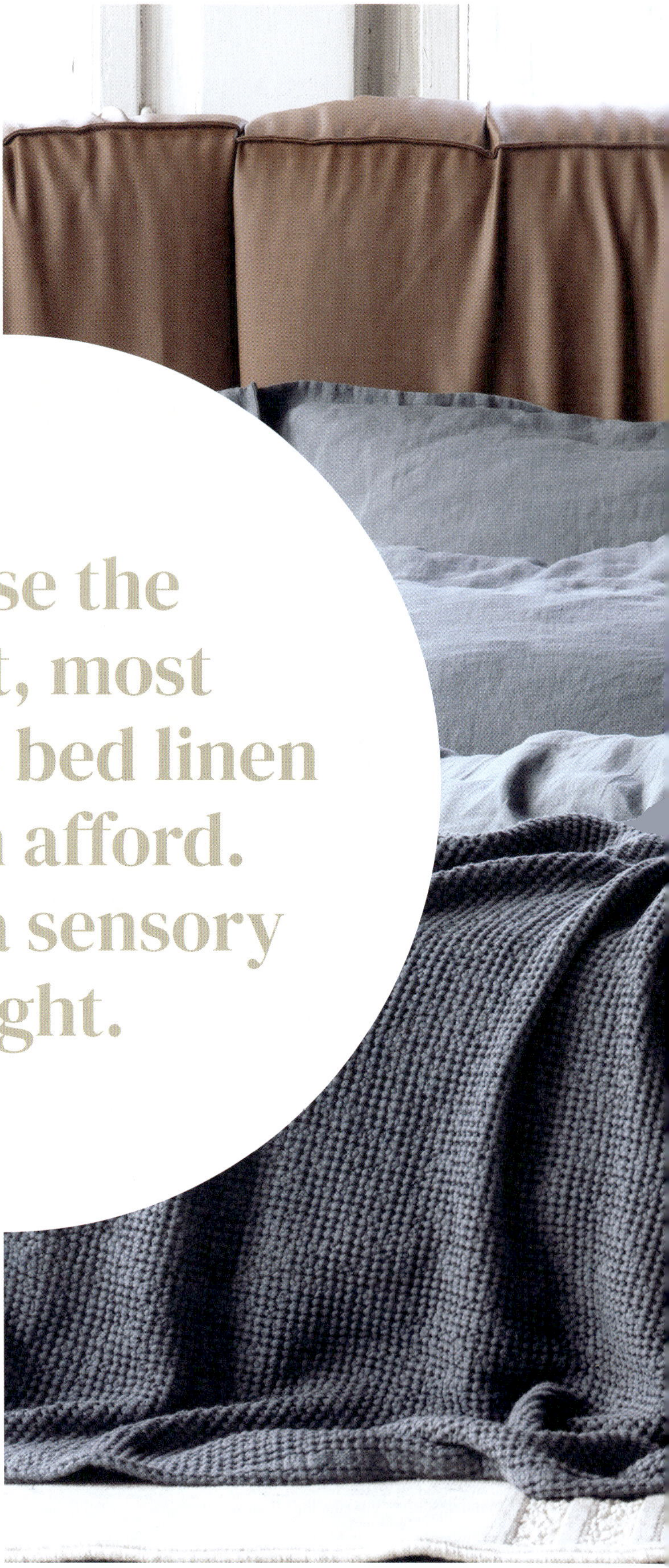

Choose the softest, most luxurious bed linen you can afford. Make it a sensory delight.

LOVE SLEEP

Be prepared to adjust your sleeping environment according to the seasons. Comfort (and the right temperature) is key to good rest and sleeping well together.

A good night's sleep maintains a speedy metabolism, increases concentration and memory, enhances creativity and makes your skin glow.

Change up your bedding for different seasons. In summer, light-weight doonas or sheets in linen or cotton and an overhead fan are essential to keep you cool, whereas in winter you'll want to snuggle down and get cosy under a much heavier doona or layers of blankets and throws.

Think about the level of humidity in your room. The optimum level for sleep is between 30 and 60%. Depending on your home environment either a dehumidifier or a diffuser can help achieve this.

Welcome plants. They improve air quality, helping to ensure that the conditions are just right for a perfect night's sleep.

Love your pillows and they will love you back. Choose wisely to promote the best night's sleep possible.

BEDSIDE YOURSELF

Pay attention to your bedside table. It's your place. Design it to promote sleep-sweet-sleep.

Invest in something beautiful that is in keeping with your design style. Keep it clean and uncluttered but add a few personal touches such as a crystal or a candle, as well as necessities like a book or Kindle, a sleep mask and hand cream. Place it at just the right distance from the bed and at the right height so that everything is within easy reach.

Select a lighting option that will keep it well lit; a bedside lamp or pendant light works really well.

Create a view in your bedroom even if you don't actually have one by introducing artwork or wallpaper that invites in the fantasy location of your dreams. If you are lucky enough to have a beautiful view, maximise it with clean windows and sheer window dressings.

Plants in the bedroom bring the space to life and improve air quality, promoting a better night's sleep. Place one large plant in the corner of the room or arrange a selection across various surfaces.

Have a place for all the things to ensure your bedroom is as clutter free and well organised as possible. A beautiful chest of drawers is both functional and stylish, providing storage space and a surface on which to display well-loved items.

Go beyond your comfort zone. Staying broadly within your design aesthetic, think about introducing lavish elements, such as darker colours, richer finishes and shimmering accents to celebrate the sensuous and create a space fit for romance.

In the bedroom, think different lighting for different purposes. Brighter lighting for dressing, and another more subtle option for reading or for when you want to create an intimate ambience.

PERSONAL TOUCHES

For optimum love, showcase the things you love and your love story.

Keep it intimate; the bedroom is not the place for photos of your kids or extended family. Instead display your favourite romantic photos of you and your partner along with treasured items from your time or travels together.

CHAPTER 4

Eating

Eat, Cook, Love

‘The people who give you their food give you their heart.’

CESAR CHAVEZ

The kitchen or dining room table is where we come together to share food and conversation, love and laughter. The gift of a meal is, for many of us, a way to express our feelings and share warmth and affection.

Our body releases dopamine when we eat delicious food, the same ‘feel-good’ chemical that is released when we look upon someone we love. So make your kitchen and dining room areas to cherish, where beautiful memories are created.

Include special touches such as handcrafted crockery, a soft rug and an elegantly dressed table with fresh flowers and linen napkins. Little details all add up to help create special moments.

Consider potted herbs and an abundant display of fresh produce to indicate the value placed on the food being made and the gifts being shared.

1. Remember functionality equals love.
Aim for simple, seamless, efficient design.

2. Light it up with easy, elegant
lighting solutions.

3. Consider open shelves for
displaying beautiful crockery.

4. A good dining table is a home's heart.

5. Don't forget about books; favourite
recipe books help tell your story.

6. Bring the outside in with potted
herbs and vibrant greenery.

7. Keep it cosy with a rug.

8. Use utensils that you love.

9. Consider tech solutions to make
life in the kitchen and dining areas
more efficient and relaxing.

10. Display items that hint at your
favourite foods and food philosophy.

Make functionality your sweetheart by creating smooth-operating kitchen and dining areas. Consider quality cutlery drawer dividers, hooks for pans or cups, beautiful storage jars or lidded bowls, a knife block or magnetic strip and stylish storage cupboards to ensure that there is a place for everything and everything is in its place.

TEA

Keep it cosy with a rug. Rugs are often overlooked in kitchens and dining areas but they are indispensable in creating warmth, comfort and that lovely luxurious feeling underfoot.

Light it up. Don't be afraid to mix and match your lighting. An eclectic range adds warmth and personality. And gives you flexibility to create the right light for all occasions.

Bring the outside in.

Make space for plants in your kitchen and dining areas. Caring for plants is known to increase levels of the happy hormone, serotonin, ensuring that there's even more love to go around your home.

Don't forget books. Displaying cookbooks filled with your favourite recipes in the kitchen and your treasured volumes in the dining area indicates your values, and adds love and heart to the home.

TABLE LOVE

The dining table is the heart of the home. Whether your space is small or large, urban or rural, the dining table is where you gather to eat, to enjoy company and conversation.

Think about what style of dining table suits your space and works with your other design choices. Long rectangular tables are best if you often host a lot of guests and round tables work well in small spaces. Whatever shape and style you choose, be it rustic, industrial, contemporary or antique, choose something that brings you joy.

Make meal times an event and celebrate the love of sharing food by paying attention to your table settings. Dress your table with charming crockery and napery, unique utensils and gorgeous glassware. Layer your crockery to create a restaurant-style look that will make your guests feel cherished. Consider placemats, tablecloths or runners and add fresh cut flowers and candles for a thoughtful touch.

Statement lighting hung low over the dining table creates an intimate ambience. Cushions or throws placed on chairs amplify the level of comfort at the table and encourage guests to linger.

Don't store Grandma's china in the top cupboard. Use the crockery, cutlery, serving dishes and wooden spoons that you love every day. Open shelving is a great option for displaying your beautiful things.

Think about technology in working spaces. An iPad stand or smart screen for recipe access comes in very handy as does a wireless charging mat. If you are renovating, consider a charging drawer in the kitchen, or pop up power points on your kitchen bench. For fabulous ambience and optimum kitchen dancing or dinner-party vibes, wireless surround sound brings in the love.

It's all about food, after all, so consider inspirational touches that reflect your food philosophy: from a well-stocked fruit bowl, to a hand coffee or flour grinder, to a display of relevant cookbooks or artwork that celebrates your eating style.

CHAPTER 5

Bathing

Home and Dry and Happy

‘Noble deeds and hot baths are the best cures for depression.’

DODIE SMITH

A hot bath or steamy shower is one of life’s simple pleasures; an experience that can soothe aching muscles and calm frazzled nerves, providing a place to rest and recharge, relax and rejuvenate.

Keep your space clear of clutter that could interfere with the serenity. Of course your bathroom needs to stock the essentials for daily ablutions, but sleek storage options can keep much of it tidied away, leaving only beautiful bottles and select objects on display.

Make a ritual of bathing, taking time to invest in yourself as you pamper, nourish and care for yourself.

Soft lighting from dimmer switches and candles helps create an intimate atmosphere, while thick, fluffy towels and luxurious accessories allow you to indulge yourself and create a space worthy of love.

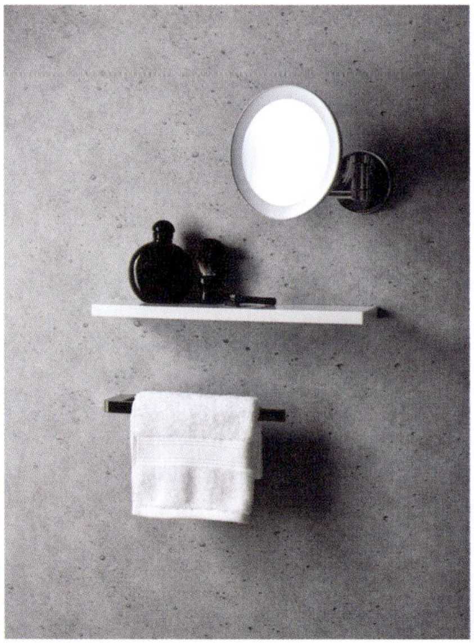

1. Select the best towels you can afford.

2. Add decorative elements such as elegant mirrors and interesting ornaments.

3. Include personal touches with small framed artworks and lush plants.

4. Replace worn out accessories such as toothbrush holders and bath mats if they begin to look less than their best.

5. Take care of your bathroom and keep it clean and dry.

6. Choose practical, sustainable love with natural soap risers and refillable bottles.

7. Select lighting that creates an intimate ambience.

8. Ensure you have sufficient hooks for towels or opt for a heated towel rail.

9. Create an everyday spa vibe with candles, slippers, towelling robes and scented oils.

10. Choose sleek storage options to keep the unsightly products hidden away.

Choose bath mats that are not only functional but also feature colours or designs that enhance the space and compliment your style to create a bathroom that is lovely and lovable.

Consider a regular revamp of your bathroom. A quick refresh, as big as a lick of paint or as small as a new soap dish, makes all the difference, ensuring your space feels fresh and cared for.

Create a spa vibe in your bathroom with fresh flowers, beautiful candles, scented oils and fluffy towelling robes and slippers. With everything set up and ready, you can feel pampered and loved, every day.

Don't overlook lighting in the bathroom. As it is a place for relaxation as well as daily maintenance, a variety of lighting options is important. A bright light near the mirror is useful, but consider a pendant light, chandelier, dimmer switches or candles as options for creating a more relaxing, ambient vibe.

soap

DECORATIVE VIBES

You don't have to do a complete remodel to show the bathroom some love. A little imagination, some time and a small budget are all that's needed to bring your decorative style to the space.

Decide on your colour palette then consider a splash of paint to the walls or pimp up an old vanity.

Coordinate your accessories, such as toothbrush holders or waste bin, and select towels, face washers and bathmats that compliment your colour scheme.

Consider mirrors and shelving with metallic accents to add glamour and a touch of romance to the space. Brass or rose gold tapware amps up that vibe.

Make a decorative feature of bath products. Seek out beautiful vintage glass containers or slick contemporary bottles to display lotions, bath salts and oils. Add beautiful bath robes and scented candles to increase the sense of a self-care haven.

An abundance of plants adds personality and freshness to the space and also helps to absorb excess moisture. Particularly good for humid climates.

Framed artworks and fresh flowers bring an extra something special that makes a bathroom seem loved and cared for, and create a space where you'll want to linger.

Ensure you have enough hooks and storage for towels. Beautiful shelving, seagrass baskets or a freestanding linen closet are great for making life easy, keeping the essentials close at hand. Consider too a heated towel rail, for that post-bath warm towel hug.

PRACTICAL, SUSTAINABLE LOVE

Choose to reuse and show your love to the planet.

There are plenty of little tips and tricks that can increase sustainability in the bathroom. Choose solid bars of soap instead of liquid soap in plastic bottles and use a soap riser to prevent your soap from disintegrating into a puddle of water. Look out for elegant cleanskin bottles (reusable bottles without labels) that can be refilled with bulk products and used over and over again. To take your cosmic love a step further, consider making your own homemade beauty products like shampoo, deodorant and soap.

In some climates certain pests love nothing more than warm, wet areas. Ensure the basics are in place, with good ventilation, an exhaust fan, and a well-fitting shower door to help your bathroom stay clean and dry and keep the pests at bay. No love lost.

The fragrance of lovely lavender is a gentle reminder of the beauty that exists in the world.

CHAPTER 6

Kids

Relax and Feel the Love

H
M
E
HOME

‘If we experienced life through the eyes of a child, everything would be magical and extraordinary.’

AKIANE KRAMARIK

Not every kid’s room can accommodate a climbing wall (though wouldn’t that be wonderful), but little touches such as cute cubbies and whimsical beds, colourful artwork or fun storage solutions add a touch of magic and a feeling of being cared for.

Create ‘invitations to play’ by setting up spaces where toys are easily accessible and displayed with intention. Kids can then explore, experiment and engage with a sense of autonomy.

Build in areas where children can retreat and tend to their own needs. Piles of cushions or beanbags for younger children and reading nooks or study spaces as the children get older.

Use plenty of colour and select soft tactile materials, taking note of the things your kids enjoy, to create love-filled rooms for kids that inspire awe and wonder.

THE ROCKS

1. Let kids participate in some decorative choices so they enjoy, respect and love the space too.

2. Prepare them for schoolwork with a desk, tech set up and shelving for books.

3. Use a colour scheme that is personal to your child, also considering the mood it creates.

4. Be sure to include design elements that reflect their passions and interests.

5. Consider wallpaper, decals or fun murals.

6. Choose smart and stylish storage options.

7. Select a bed that is beautiful and inviting.

8. Include durable elements that will stand the test of time.

9. Allow space for self-governance with locking drawers and diaries and cubbies to hide in.

10. Opt for plenty of comfortable seating: beanbags, poufs, fold-out loungers and swivel chairs to help get their wiggles out.

Whether it's pops of colour
on a neutral canvas or bold
feature walls, colour brings
love, life and joy to a kid's
bedroom.

Bring in a sense of whimsy that reflects your kid's interests. Whether that's showcasing their artistic talents with some of their framed creations, a Lego display unit or a climbing wall. Whatever your kid's passion may be, show it some love.

GREAT
MR.FOX
COMING SOON
in the
forest

LOVE SECRETS

All kids need to be able to safely conceal themselves or their secrets. Give them the chance to do just that.

Make space for cubbies, teepees and dens. Kids' soft furniture that can be taken apart and rebuilt in various forms is a great idea and offers endless opportunities for play. Consider drawers they can lock and diaries with padlocks, which encourage safe secret-keeping to foster a sense of independence and power.

Involve your child in the design of their room and they will feel proud of the space.

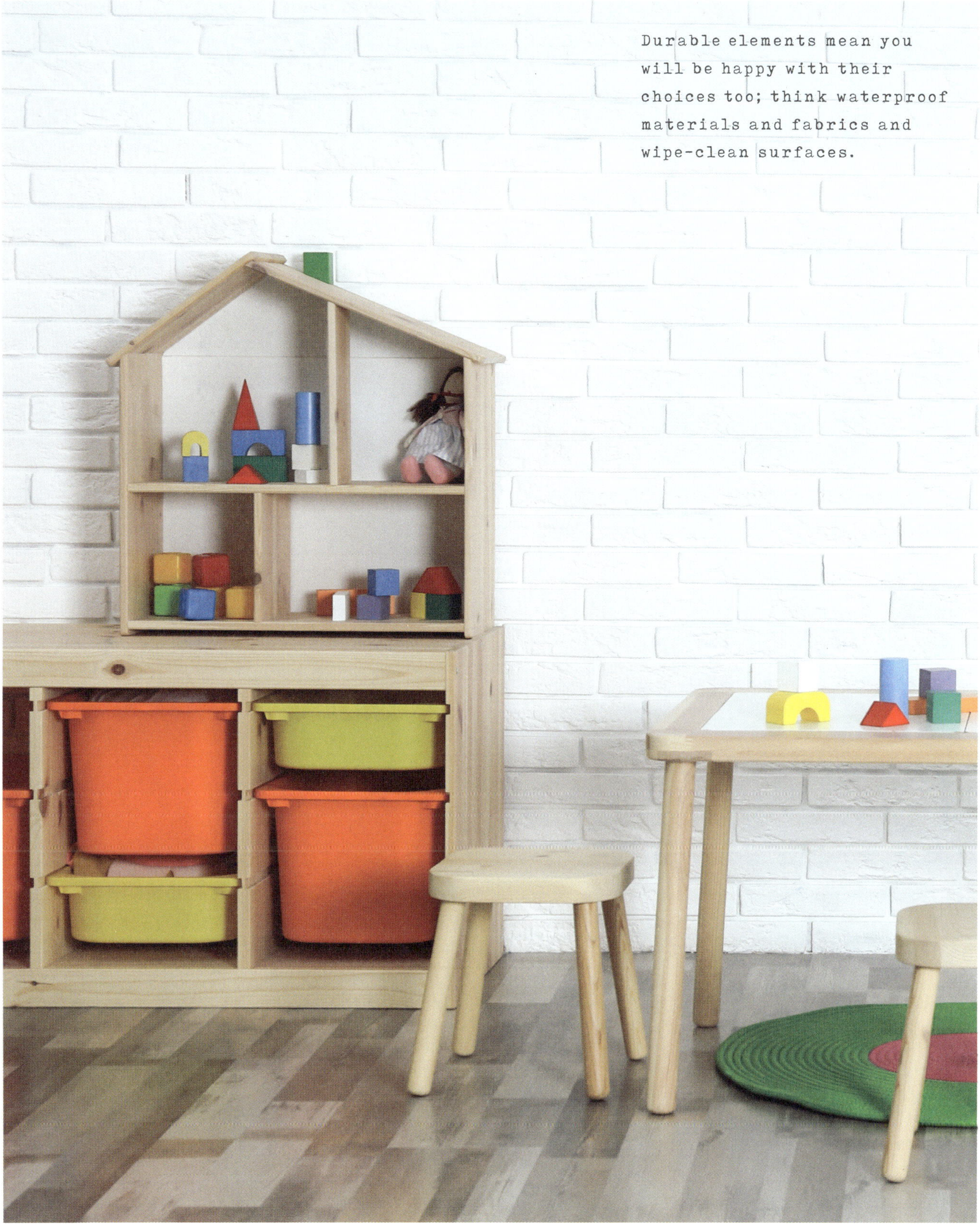

Durable elements mean you will be happy with their choices too; think waterproof materials and fabrics and wipe-clean surfaces.

Don't touch my stuff!

Storage, storage and more storage. Kids have stuff and kids' stuff has stuff. It can easily build up, so ensure you make provisions with well-planned storage for clothes, schoolwork, toys and trinkets.

Feature walls are a great way to add joy and heart to a kid's room. Think fun wallpaper, painted murals or transfers to create dynamic, well-loved spaces.

LOVE COMFORT

All kids love a place to kick back and relax in the bedroom. Depending on the space, that could be a lazy fold-out lounger, a pouf, beanbag, or perhaps a swivel chair or swing for kids that need to wriggle their wiggles out.

Kids love to explore the sensation of touch so layer the bed with soft bed linen, blankets and throws in rich tactile materials like velvet, that they will love to snuggle up in and stroke.

Children spend a lot of time down on the floor so choose thick rugs and sheepskins, perfect to sink little toes into, and have plenty of cushions and pillows available in cosy corners, which can double up as cubby building materials.

The feeling of comfort can also come from gentle ambient lighting such as salt lamps, fairy lights or night lights that project twinkling stars onto the ceiling. Choosing pastel colours creates a calming environment that helps induce rest and relaxation.

Using soft fabrics as a decorative tool for things like storage hampers, bed canopies and macrame wall hangings brings in an element of cosiness that makes a space feel warm and inviting.

Don't forget about soft toys. An abundance of plush soft toys and fun, theme-shaped cushions provides plenty of opportunities for cuddles and the loving sensation of being held.

The bed is an important statement, so make sure it's the right shape and size, whether they are big or small. Decorate it with their personality in mind and make it a beautiful place to rest, relax and sleep.

Older kids benefit from a dedicated space for their schoolwork. A nice, uncluttered place to work with good lighting and a place for everything helps to set them up for success.

"It's a wonderous thing, how the wild calms the child."

ANON

Create some calm among the chaos with elements of nature, in the form of plant motifs, fresh foliage or wildlife photography.

Encourage your teenager to create a vision board. Pepper it with positive affirmations, photos and things they love. This helps them remember where they are heading and what they hold dear.

CHAPTER 7

Outdoors

Nurture Nature

‘Another glorious day, the air as delicious to the lungs as nectar to the tongue.’

JOHN MUIR

Spending time outdoors is one of life’s great joys and one of the many ways we can choose to love and care for ourselves, as it lowers stress, boosts immunity and improves sleep quality.

You don’t need a huge expanse of garden to reap the benefits of spending time in nature. Tending to a window box or a small balcony vegetable garden allows you to observe the seasons shift and provides an equal opportunity to enjoy the fruits of your labour.

In designing your outside space, be sure to include areas designated to the things that bring you the most pleasure, be that sipping a glass of wine at sunset or greeting the day with a morning yoga routine.

Maximise the space you have, taking advantage of the most desirable aspects for each season. Design your space with care and bask in the deliciousness of time spent outside.

1. Make sure you have plenty of shade so you can relax in comfort.

2. Use ambient lighting at night and make the most of natural light throughout the day.

3. Choose comfortable seating, positioned with the most desirable aspect in mind.

4. Build in places to eat and share food.

5. Create 'moments', each with a specific focus.

6. Make it a space for all seasons, with shade and fans for summer, screens and fire pits in winter.

7. Don't forget the details. Give as much love to your outdoor spaces as to the inside of your home.

8. Choose fixtures and furnishings that are weather resistant and easily cleanable.

9. Stay cool with an outdoor bath or shower.

10. Build a veggie patch or flower garden and learn to love the seasons.

Shade covering is essential in this climate but it doesn't need to be elaborate or expensive. Plants can provide shade for free, or low-cost options like sun umbrellas (multiple, pretty ones perhaps) do a great job too.

Cooking and eating outdoors makes everything taste better. Give thought to making your barbecue area as user-friendly (and clean) as possible. If you have an outdoor kitchen, treat it with as much love and attention as you would your indoor kitchen.

Position your outdoor living spaces to make the best of your home's aspect and of the natural light that flows your way.

Life is better around an open fire. Create one in your own backyard and save on the stress of going camping!

Love the outdoors at your place. Create a comfy place to kick back with plenty of cushions and padded seating.

LOVE MOMENTS

Even if you only have a small outdoor space it's possible to create 'moments'. which simply means having a different focus for different areas.

In a larger garden you might be able to create a moment for relaxation with a hanging chair, a moment for gardening with a veggie patch, a moment for relaxing with soft outdoor furniture (and a glass of chilled wine), and a moment for quiet contemplation with a Buddha statue or other soul zone.

In a small space, a designated chair for your morning cuppa, a compact barbecue for outdoor cooking or a small window box for gardening work just as well.

Consider the things that you love and the ways that you most enjoy living when creating these spaces. If you enjoy entertaining be sure to include an area that can accommodate guests, and if you like curling up with a book, a cosy outdoor chair with weatherproof cushions makes for a lovely spot.

Outdoor 'moments' can be divided up using lush greenery or with wooden or bamboo screens, or they can simply flow organically into one another.

Consider the change of seasons when designing these spaces. Perhaps a fire pit in winter can be moved out to make way for a shaded dining table in summer or a heated outdoor bath can transform to cold plunge pool as the seasons shift.

Ensure adequate shade, heating or protection for each space, maximising comfort, for moments you can really fall in love with.

An outdoor bath or shower is a treat and a joy. The bath provides the perfect place for a romantic scene, so, if you are lucky enough to have one, make it beautiful and enjoy it.

Show your guests some love with beautiful crockery and elaborate table settings. Take time to make your entertaining areas beautiful and create special moments using the best of everything.

Don't overlook decorative details in your outdoor space. Is there a spot for a small water feature or statue? Maybe display gardenware that fits your style and holds meaning for you.

Home-grown herbs and veggies are economical, practical and aromatic but moreover add a hard-to-put-your-finger-on element of joy and love to life and home. Also consider cultivating a small flower garden so you always have hand-cut blooms available for decoration.

Consider what you need to make your outdoor space feel the love year-round. Add a fire pit or gas heater for winter and provide plenty of shade for summer.

String lighting creates a festive feeling that you can enjoy all year-round.

Illuminate different outdoor areas with various lighting options. Highlight specific plants with spotlights, use walkway lighting on pathways and create an ambient mood in entertaining or relaxing areas with festoon lighting or lanterns.

HERRON
First Published in 2023 by Herron Book Distributors Pty Ltd
14 Manton St
Morningside
QLD 4170
www.herronbooks.com

Captain Honey
WWW.CAPTAINHONEY.COM.AU

Custom book production by Captain Honey Pty Ltd
12 Station Street
Bangalow
NSW 2479
www.captainhoney.com.au

Cataloguing-in-Publication. A catalogue record for this book is available from the National Library of Australia

ISBN 978-1-922944-34-4

Printed and bound in China

5 4 3 2 1 23 24 25 26 27